Published by Creative Education
and Creative Paperbacks
P.O. Box 227, Mankato, Minnesota 56002
Creative Education and Creative Paperbacks
are imprints of The Creative Company
www.thecreativecompany.us

Design by The Design Lab
Production by Travis Green
Art direction by Rita Marshall
Printed in the United States of America

Photographs by Alamy (louise murray, WorlFoto), Corbis (Radius Images, Paul Souders, Michelle Valberg/All Canada Photos), National Geographic Creative (PAUL NICKLEN), Shutterstock (Hal Brindley, Vladimir Melnik), SuperStock (Minden Pictures, NaturePL)

Library of Congress Cataloging-in-Publication Data
Bodden, Valerie.
Walruses / Valerie Bodden.
p. cm. — (Amazing animals)
Summary: A basic exploration of the appearance, behavior, and habitat of walruses, the Arctic pinnipeds with whiskers. Also included is a story from folklore explaining why walruses have tusks.
Includes bibliographical references and index.
ISBN 978-1-60818-615-0 (hardcover)
ISBN 978-1-62832-221-7 (pbk)
ISBN 978-1-56660-662-2 (eBook)
1. Walrus—Juvenile literature. I. Title. II. Series: Amazing animals.
QL737.P62B63 2016
599.79'9—dc23   2014048716

CCSS: RI.1.1, 2, 4, 5, 6, 7; RI.2.2, 5, 6, 7, 10; RI.3.1, 5, 7, 8; RF.1.1, 3, 4; RF.2.3, 4

HC 9 8 7 6 5 4 3 2
First Edition PBK 9 8 7 6 5 4 3 2 1

AMAZING ANIMALS

WALRUSES

BY VALERIE BODDEN

CREATIVE EDUCATION • CREATIVE PAPERBACKS

A walrus's body helps it stay warm in the cold water

Walruses are animals called pinnipeds. That means they are sea **mammals** that have **flippers**. Seals and sea lions are pinnipeds, too.

flippers wide, flat body parts that walruses use for swimming and walking

mammals animals that have hair or fur and feed their babies with milk

A walrus uses its tusks to climb onto ice, fight, and more

Walruses have two front flippers and two back flippers. Their long, thick bodies are covered with wrinkly, brown skin. They have small eyes, big **tusks**, and more than 400 whiskers.

tusks big, pointed teeth that stick out of the mouth

Walruses can be 7.5 to 11.5 feet (2.3–3.5 m) long. Male walruses can weigh up to 3,700 pounds (1,678 kg). That is as much as a car! Females weigh about half as much as males.

Walruses have a thick layer of fat under their skin

Walruses may dive off sea ice to catch their food

Walruses live in **Arctic** seas. Every year, walruses **migrate**. In the summer, they stay far to the north. In the winter, they move toward the south. But they always stay near sea ice.

Arctic an area at the top of Earth where no trees grow

migrate move from place to place during different parts of the year

Walruses eat crabs, clams, starfish, and sea cucumbers. Sometimes they eat fish or small seals. Walruses can eat 100 pounds (45.4 kg) of food a day!

A walrus's front flipper has five short digits, or fingers

*Walrus calves go
for rides on their
mothers' backs*

A mother walrus gives birth to one **calf** every two years. The calf can swim almost as soon as it is born. Female calves sometimes stay with their mother's **herd** their whole lives. But male calves leave their mothers when they are five or six years old. Walruses can live up to 40 years.

calf a baby walrus

herd a group of walruses that live together

Walruses spend most of their time in the water. They use their whiskers to feel for food on the seafloor. But they come to the surface to breathe air. Walruses can stay underwater for 25 minutes.

Most walruses do not often dive deeper than 262 feet (80 m)

When they are not in the water, walruses gather on the ice or land. A group of walruses can be noisy! Walruses grunt, groan, bark, and snort.

Walruses in a herd like to stay close to one another

People around the world love walruses. Many people see them in zoos. Other people travel to see them in the wild. It can be fun to watch these big sea animals sleep, swim, and walk on their flippers!

Walruses usually swim about 4.3 miles (6.9 km) per hour

A Walrus Story

Why do walruses have tusks? People in Alaska used to tell a story about this. They said Old Man and Old Woman made all the animals. One day, Old Man made a caribou with tusks. Old Woman made a walrus with antlers. But the animals were too hard to hunt. So Old Man and Old Woman changed them. From then on, the caribou had antlers, and the walrus had tusks.

Read More

Johnson, Jinny. *Polar Sea Life*. Mankato, Minn.: Smart Apple Media, 2012.

Sexton, Colleen. *Walruses*. Minneapolis: Bellwether Media, 2008.

Websites

Enchanted Learning: Walrus
http://www.enchantedlearning.com/subjects/mammals/pinniped/Walrusprintout.shtml
This site has walrus facts and a picture to color.

National Geographic Kids: Walrus
http://kids.nationalgeographic.com/content/kids/en_US/animals/walrus/
Learn lots more facts about walruses.

Note: Every effort has been made to ensure that the websites listed above are suitable for children, that they have educational value, and that they contain no inappropriate material. However, because of the nature of the Internet, it is impossible to guarantee that these sites will remain active indefinitely or that their contents will not be altered.

Index